The Return of
HOW TO TALK TEXAN

BY
"CRAZY"
JOHN FARRELL 1986

Revived by ALBERT HENDERSON 2011/2019

Author's original disclaimer:

This book is written only in good humor
and not meant in any way to offend anybody.
I had a blast writing this book and I really
hope you get a real TEXAS kick out of reading it.

Thanks a meeyen...
"Crazy" John Farrell
5/1/86

25 years later John's humor lives again!!
The Return of
How to Talk Texan
Revived by Albert Henderson
In memory of
JOHN JOSEPH FARRELL

Special thanks to my wife, Pat, who was a
great help with editing (of course, not the TEXAN!!)
Special thanks also to my son, Shawn, and our friend
Shannon Hebert, who provided invaluable technical
support. Thanks also to John's sister, Katrina, for
giving permission to republish this book and for
spotting many of my errors.

Thank you God, for giving us John
and all of his talents.

IN LOVING MEMORY OF
JOHN JOSEPH FARRELL
February 14, 1944-January 21, 2010

Here is what John Originally said:
This book is dedicated to my
Beloved grandfather,
OSCAR HENDERSON
1886-1970
who enjoyed practical jokes
and good humor.

The Story behind

<u>The Return of How to Talk Texan</u>

By Albert Don Henderson

After John was diagnosed with pancreatic cancer in 2009, we all knew his time on this Earth short. Fortunately or unfortunately, depending on how you look at it; John was not able to completely comprehend everything due to the head injury he received in an automobile accident. This occurred as he was returning to his home after Hurricane Ike had caused a power outage. Because of his accident; he became a nursing home resident. A part of the old John remained, but not all. For those who knew John; know that he possessed extraordinary talents; especially when it came to business.

The following is a list of just a few of the things that John was able to accomplish during his life time. John was on the high school golf teams in Ft. Worth and Houston, he caddied for Ben Hogan, started the first golf team at HCJC (now Trinity Valley Jr. College), had a column in the college newspaper, sold real-estate in Houston and Austin, helped run a pool hall in Malakoff, Texas, worked for a swimming pool company in Houston, owned a swimming pool company in Houston, named Who's Who in Texas, 1976, listed in the Houston Chronicle Bicentennial Vignettes of American History(1976), owned three different pawn shops, owned and operated "The Loose Goose Salon", owned and operated two "Beer-Joints" on Bolivar Island, wrote a book, owned a golf shop, taught golf, was an artist, and much more. All in all, God gave John a rainbow of talents, which he used in many different aspects of life. John wrote and put together his book: <u>How to Talk Texan</u> in 1986; the same year as the 150th anniversary of Texas independence. It seemed only fitting that a new book should be released. Most of the original has been maintained with loving care.

Now, 33 years later, in honor of John Farrell and Texas Independence:

<u>The Return of How to Talk Texan;</u> 1986-2019

<u>Texas Independence,</u> 183 years; 1836-2019

PODNA. . .
a person of
close
relationship
or
friend.

"Howdy
PODNA
welcome to
Texas."

CHAMPEEN.....

to win it all,
to be number one

**WURLD
SERIES
CHAMPEEN
ASTROS**

**Ah am
so proud of
the ASTROS
ah am
bustin
my
vest**

STRACK . . .
a swing and a miss
in baseball; to
swing and miss
a baseball.

**STRACK
three
you're
OUT!!**

must be
Verlander
Pitching!!
Go Astros!!

MESKIN...
a person of
Spanish descent,
who has brown
skin and probably
lives south of the
border.

"When ah was in
Ackapuco, a
MESKIN told mae
that if there had
been a back door
to the Alamo
there wouldn't
have been a
Texas, and ah'm
mad."

MAIRD...
to engage in
wedlock.

"Son, muh
daughter is
pragnant and
if she ain't
MAIRD
by noon today
yore gonna see
daylight through
yore rear."

AWL . . .
a thick black
underground
liquid.

"Muh **AWL** wells
have made mae
one rich Texan,
the fact is ah'm
a multi-meeyenar."

6

WRAL . . .
a large metal bar
usually made out of
arn and is used
as a support.

"Our sheriff
runs crooks out
of town on a
WRAL."

RACK . . .to destroy or go to pieces; to devastate.

"Back TAXES
and the IR-ASS
Audit is
making mae
a nervous
RACK!"

BAIRD ...
hidden; or to completely cover up.

"Ya'll dig here, ah thank I've found the **BAIRD** treasure.!"

AIRS . . .
an opening, used for hearing located on each side of a persons head.

"Speak up mam ah kain't hear you 'cause muh **AIRS** are stopped up."

FARRY . . .
as in children's
nursery
rhines.

"**FARRY** tales ain't
just for kids,
you know."

WHEECH . . .
of what
direction.

"Do ya'll know
WHEECH
way is the
restrums?"

TAIRS . . .
salty water that
comes out of the
eyes when a person
is sad.

"Just mention the
ALAMO and it
brangs TAIRS to
muh eyes."

TACK . . .
a blood-sucking
varmit of the
insect
family.

"This here
TACK is
so begg ah
nicknamed
him
Dracula."

FRAZE...
to be very, very, cold.

"The travel agent said Alaska was warm in July but ah'm 'bout to **FRAZE** muh buns off."

UNNER-YUNNER...
underneath and
overthere.

"There he is,
UNNER-YUNNER!"

ARN . . .
a very strong metal, steel-like.

"Muh arms are
as strong
as **ARN.**

CORNFUSED...
an exasperating
state of
mind.

"I'm so
CORNFUSED
ah kain't make
muh mind up if
I should or
shouldn't"

FEAL . . .
a plot of ground
with grass used
to play a sporting
game.

Ya-hoo, here
comes the
HOUSTON TEXANS
out on the
FEAL!"

Misunderestimate......

not giving a person
enough credit

The Cowboys
**MISUNDER-
ESTIMATED**

mah ability
when Ah
tried out!!

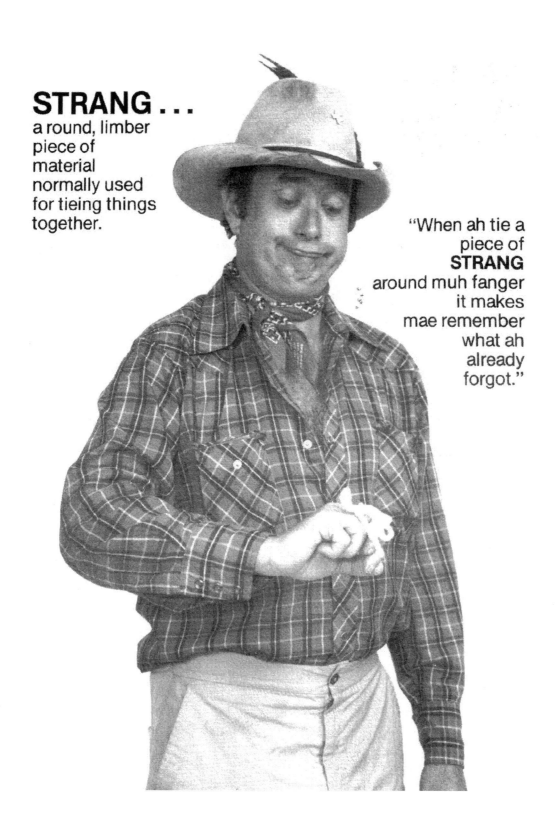

STRANG . . .

a round, limber piece of material normally used for tieing things together.

"When ah tie a piece of **STRANG** around muh fanger it makes mae remember what ah already forgot."

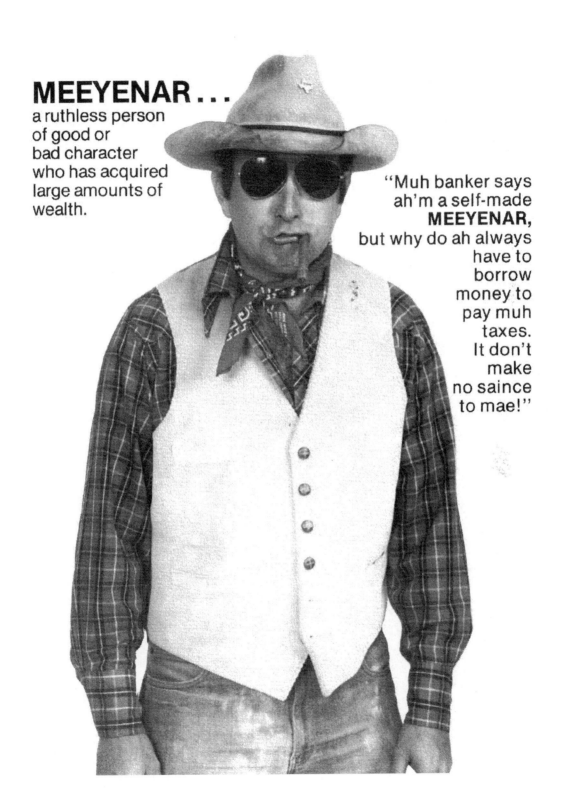

MEEYENAR...

a ruthless person
of good or
bad character
who has acquired
large amounts of
wealth.

"Muh banker says
ah'm a self-made
MEEYENAR,
but why do ah always
have to
borrow
money to
pay muh
taxes.
It don't
make
no saince
to mae!"

CHATE...
to underhandedly
displace someone
out of their money.

"When ah play poker
with the big boys,
ah don't **CHATE,**
but ah wonna make
sure if ah
have to
ah can."

MANE...
a person of
tough
character.

"That thar feller
is as **MANE** as a
red-headed stepchild."

BARLY . . .
of a small
amount;
or
minute.

"Ah'm so tard
ah can
BARLY
hold mah
eyes
open."

QUAR . . .
a coordinated
group of singers.

"Ah have been
chosen to sang
in the **QUAR.**"

SAK . . .
bad condition of
ones' health,
especially
mental anxiety.

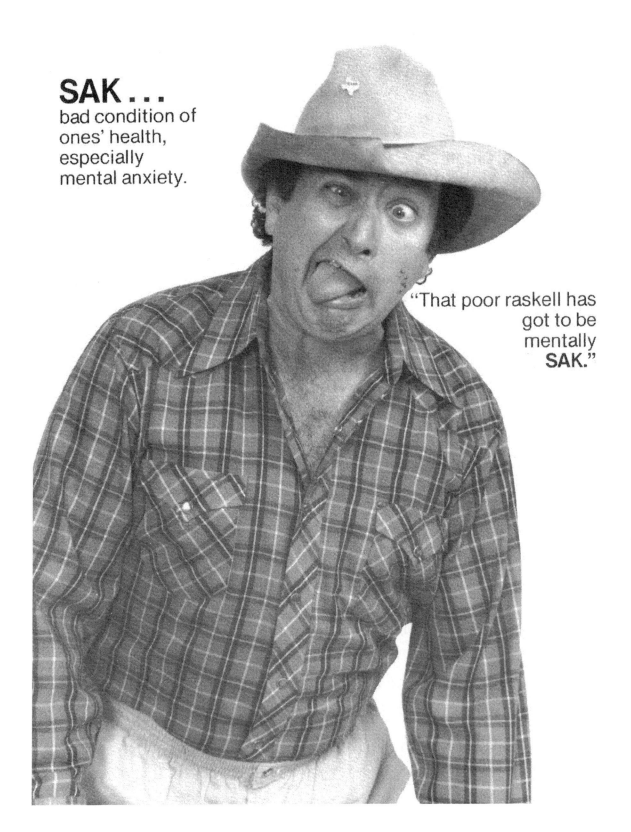

"That poor raskell has
got to be
mentally
SAK."

SEP . . .
instead of.

"Ah'd play
football for
the Dallis
Cowboys,

SEP . . .
Jerry
ain't hirin
right now!!"

FIXIN TO.....

About to, going to
Ah wuz
FIXIN TO
try out with
the Dynamo,
but they sed
I brung the wrong
kind of football.
Ah thought thir
wuz only one
kind of football in
Texas

WUSH ...
to hope something
or anything would
turn out in your
favor.

"Ah ain't much
on gambling
but ah **WUSH**
muh bookie
would lose
just once."

HAIR...
an adverb meaning
in or to this
place.

"Ah said, come
HAIR
right now."

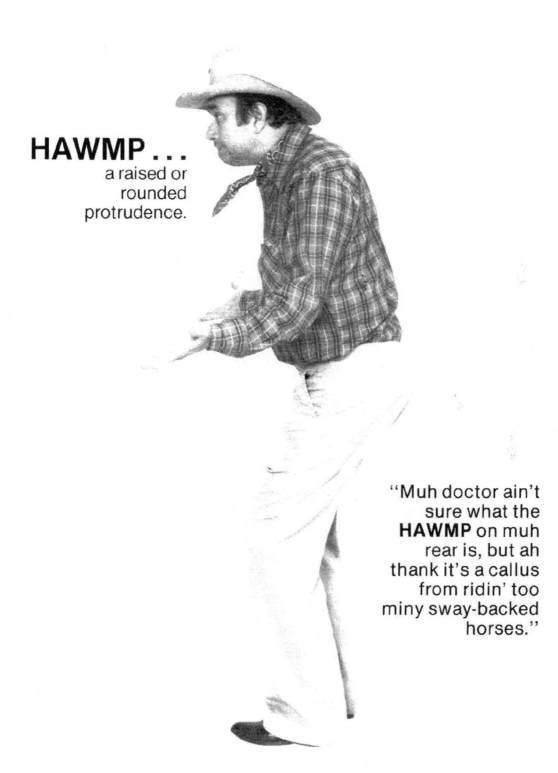

HAWMP...
a raised or
rounded
protrudence.

"Muh doctor ain't
sure what the
HAWMP on muh
rear is, but ah
thank it's a callus
from ridin' too
miny sway-backed
horses."

POM'S...
the underside of
a persons
hands.

"If ah bend muh
nays ah kin touch
muh **POMS**
evertime.

BORRY . . .
to make or ask
for a loan from
a person.

"Mister, could ah
BORRY a dime,
'cause ah ain't ett
in three days."

BEGG . . .
of giant
size.

"The waves here
in Hona Lulu,
Hawayer are
almost as
BEGG
as those in
Galveston."

PRANCE...

a person of nobility. High ranking official.

"The **PRANCE** of Saudi Arabia wants to mate with mae on a begg multi-meeyen dollar awl deal."

RAGLER . . .
to be very
consistent; or
recurring at
specific times.

Muh doctor told
me that ah
was in good
health
'cause
ah'm
a very
RAGLER
guy

PANK...
a color opsite
of blue that
most
men hate
and most
women like.

"When ah was in
San Francisco
Californyer,
ah actually
seen a
growed up
man
wearing a
PANK
SUIT
WITH
PANK
shoes."

RETARD.........

when a person doesn't work anymore.

Ah ainit goin' to lift a fanger anymore 'cause a'm

RETARD

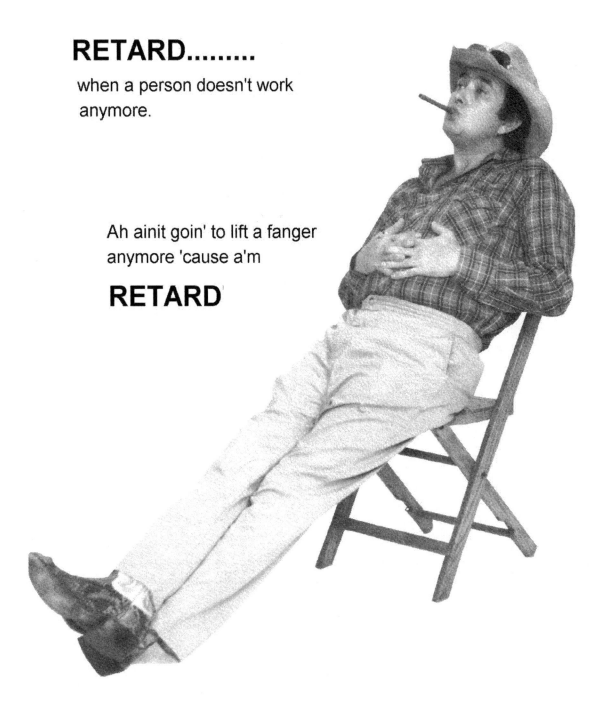

PAILS . . .

a small tablet
of medicine
to be
swallowed

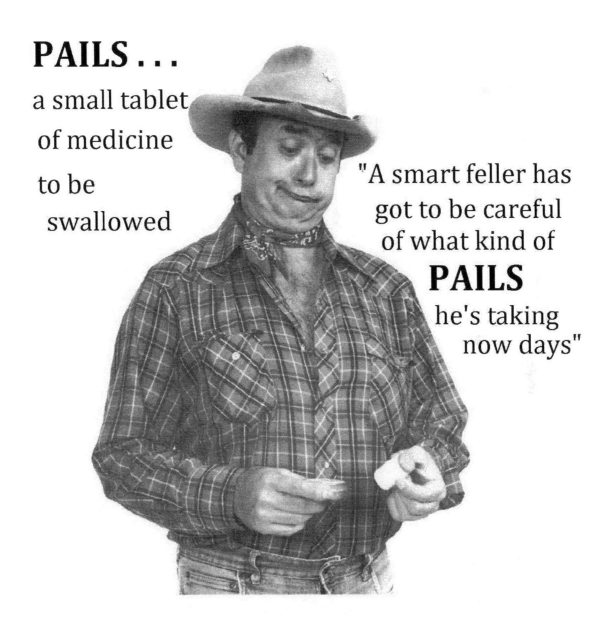

"A smart feller has
got to be careful
of what kind of
PAILS
he's taking
now days"

BRANK...
near the edge;
a nervous
condition.

"Ah thank ah'm
on the **BRANK**
of a nervous
breakdown."

AFAR...

to have a secret
relationship
with a person
of the opsit
sex, without
yore spouse
knowing

"There's no reason
at all for muh
wife to suspect
mae of having
an **AFAR**
with the widder
woman."

PIRE...
to have super
strength;
mechanical-like
ability.

Even Tiger Sez
Ah have super

......PIRE

FAIR . . .
to be scared
half to death;
pure fright.

"When muh awl
wells start
pumpin'
saltwater
'stead of
awl, it
strikes
the **FAIR** of God
in mae."

44

JAL . . .
a place with bars
where criminals
are confined
for extended
periods of
time.

"Judge, please don't
send me to **JAL**
just 'cause ah
drank too
much and
drove off
in the
wrong
Cadillac.
'Sides that,
muh keys
fit."

GRANE...
the color of grass.

"When ah git fightin'
mad muh face
turns purple and
then
GRANE."

SAINCE . . .
to have or not to
have mental
intelligence;
a state of
mind.

"That there feller
ain't got no
SAINCE
at all!"

SIRE . . .
a very tart and
tangy taste.

"Muh Aint Maries
lemonade is so
SIRE it makes muh
whole body
pucker."

BAILS . . .

the windowed envelope letters sent in the mail by your creditors, that ain't never welcome and are always due.

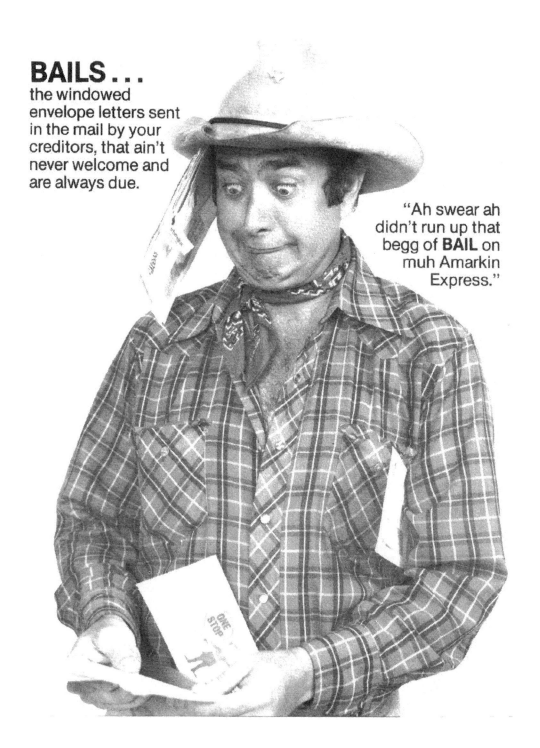

"Ah swear ah didn't run up that begg of **BAIL** on muh Amarkin Express."

BLONN . . .
a person that can't see.

"Ah may be
BLONN but
ah ain't stupid."

JAGALOW ...
a man that doesn't work
and lives off
a woman's money.

"At one time in muh
life, a person could
have called me
a **JAGALOW**."

FLIERS

a plant
with blooms that
normally smells
good and makes
most women
happy.

"Hi Honey
ah know yore
mad at mae, but
I brung ye some
FLIERS anyway."

GUFF . . .
the ocean border-
ing Texas and
Mexico.

"In muh opinion
they need to change
the name of the
GUFF of Mexico to
the **GUFF** of Texas."

MATE...
to introduce
ones self or
to know
someone.

"See ya'll later,
it shor was nice
to **MATE** ye."

GLOSSARY

AFAR...Affair
AH...I
AH'M...I'm
AINT...Aunt
AIRS...Ears
AMARKIN...American
ARN...Iron
AST...Asked
AWL...Oil
BAIRD...Buried
BAILS...Bills
BORRY..BORROW
BARLY...Barely
BEGG...Big
BIDNESS...Business
BLONN...Blind
BRANK...Brink
CHATE...Cheat
CORNFUSED.. Confused
ETT...Ate
FAIR...Fear
FANGER...Finger
FARRY...Fairy
FASH...Fish
FEAL...Field
FRAZE...Freeze
GOFF...Golf
GRANE...Green
GUFF... Gulf
HAIR...Here
HAWMP...Hump
HITE...Hyatt
JAGALOW.. Gigolo
JAL...Jail
KIN—Can
MAE...Me
MANE...Mean
MAIRD...Married
MATE...Meet
MEEYENAR...Millionaire
MESKIN...Mexican
MISUNDERESTIMATE... Under Estimate

MUH...My
NAYS...Knees
PAILS...Pills
PANK...Pink
PAPLE...People
PIRE... Power
PODNA...Partner
POMS...Palms
PRANCE...Prince
QUAR...Choir
RACK... Wreck
RAGLER...Regular
RESTRUMS...Rest Rooms
REFUDIATE..Repudiate
RETARD...Retired
SAINCE...Since
SAK...Sick
SANG...Sing
SEP... Except
SEPTAQUINTAQUIN-
QUECENTENNIAL... 175th
Anniversary
SHOR...Sure
SIRE...Sour
STEAD...Instead
STRACK...Strike
STRANG...String
SWANG...Swing
TACK... Tick
TAIRS...Tears
TARD...Tired
THANK...Think
UNNER-YUNNER...Under
Yonder
WINDER...Widow
WRAL...Rail
WONNA...Want TO
WHEECH...Which
WUSH...Wish
YA'11...You All
YORE... Your

About the Author . . .

"CRAZY" JOHN FARRELL,

Pulit Surprize winner and known as the man of a meeyen faces. One
of his lifetime desires is to have his picture on a national stamp. He is a
master genius of humor-
ous situations. His ability
to make people laugh
is known throughout large
parts of deserted Texas
wastelands and other des-
olate areas. An unknown
Wine-O called him the
Will Rogers of the 1980's.
The two dozen or so men-
tal midgets who have
bought and read
"How to Talk Texan"
have laughed their little arses off.
"WE HOPE YOU DID TOO!"

**PULIT SURPRIZE
WINNER**, a rare
Photograph of the
Author, "Crazy John Farrell"
Shown holding his **PULIT SURPRIZE AWARD**

John Farrell (Right) listed in the 1976 Bicentennial issue of the
Houston Chronicle, President of Nassau Pools in Houston

JOHN JOSEPH FARRELL
A RAINBOW OF TALENTS
February 14, 1944- January 21, 2010

CRAZY JOHN SHARES SOME TEXAS HISTORY

- <u>March 2nd 1836</u>:Texas Declaration of Independence signed at the Republic of Texas Convention and a new interim Republic of Texas was formed

- <u>March 6, 1836</u>: The Alamo under Col. William B. Travis overwhelmed by the Mexican army after a 2 week siege

- <u>March 10, 1836</u>: Sam Houston retreats to avoid advancing Mexican army

- <u>March 27, 1836</u>: James Fannin and 400 Texans executed at the Goliad Massacre

- <u>April 21, 1836</u>: Under the leadership of Sam Houston The Texans whip Santa Anna and the Mexican at San Jacinto

- <u>November 1839</u>: The Texas Congress met in Austin and selected Austin as the capital of the New Republic

MADE IN TEXAS BY
A TEXAN

CONGRATULATIONS ASTROS

WORLD SERIES CHAMPS 2017

Made in the USA
Coppell, TX
16 December 2022

89332541R00037